Consider Some Flowers

poems by

Keena Boling

Finishing Line Press
Georgetown, Kentucky

Consider Some Flowers

For Todd, Margaux & Weezie

In Memoriam
Christian McDonald
1983-2002

Copyright © 2020 by Keena Boling
ISBN 978-1-64662-275-7 First Edition
All rights reserved under International and Pan-American Copyright Conventions. No part of this book may be reproduced in any manner whatsoever without written permission from the publisher, except in the case of brief quotations embodied in critical articles and reviews.

ACKNOWLEDGMENTS

The epigraphs for parts I, II, and III are from the chapter "The Glass Flowers" page 224 from the book *Things That Talk: Object Lessons from Art and Science* edited by Lorraine J. Daston (New York: Zone Books, 2004).

"Secret Apparatus": Italicized line from "Introduction" page 8 from the book *The Glass Flowers at Harvard* by Richard Evans Schultes and William A. Davis (New York: E.P. Dutton, 1982).

Information about the Blaschkas and the Glass Flowers are from *Drawing Upon Nature: Studies for the Blaschkas' Glass Models* selected and introduced by Susan M. Rossi-Wilcox and David Whitehouse (New York: The Corning Museum of Glass, 2007), *Things That Talk: Object Lessons from Art and Science,* and *The Glass Flowers at Harvard.*

"Nine Feet": Italicized line from the closing strophe of Charles Wright's poem "Portrait of the Artist with Li Po" from *The Southern Cross* (New York: Random House, 1981).

Two poems appeared in the following publications:
an earlier version of "Most Days" in *The Writing Disorder*
"The Season of Necessary Intimacy" in *Into the Teeth of the Wind*

Publisher: Leah Maines
Editor: Christen Kincaid
Cover Art: Collection of the Rakow Research Library, The Corning Museum of Glass, Corning, NY
Author Photo: Sam Oates
Cover Design: Elizabeth Maines McCleavy

Order online: www.finishinglinepress.com
also available on amazon.com

Author inquiries and mail orders:
Finishing Line Press
P. O. Box 1626
Georgetown, Kentucky 40324
U. S. A.

Table of Contents

I.

The Season of Necessary Intimacy 1

The First Sign of Dying 2

Returning to an Empty House 3

After Death 4

II.

Relics of Glass 7

The Passion Flower 8

Most Days 9

The Water Lilies 10

Consider Some Flowers 11

III.

Ghost Plant 15

Nine Feet 16

Secret Apparatus 17

And I Am Reminded How We Slept 18

How to Define Things 19

What I Tell the Worktable 20

Without 21

I

*The triumph of all artistic naturalism,
the successful deception of the senses.*

THE SEASON OF NECESSARY INTIMACY

Somewhere shadows
scavenge the island.

They tongue the ribs
of hydrangea plants,

insensitive
to empty homes,

empty moors,
gulls

that suture sky
and stilt houses.

This morning
the harbor froze.

The last fishing boats
motionless, frosted

hulls, abandoned
fishing twine.

THE FIRST SIGN OF DYING

It is customary for the feet to go cold first
the hospice nurse says. The cold moves upwards,
spreads like the tide. I wait
for the morphine. I sit until evening.
Rising occasionally to check.
Palm on sole. Palm on heel. Again
and again and again.

RETURNING TO AN EMPTY HOUSE

I take off my coat.
Make coffee. Feed the dog.
Say *Nothing inside this house is the same.*
Explain to the specimens
How I wanted to hold
your hand one last time,
but your hand was too pale.
It would have felt unlike you.

AFTER DEATH

At first I drew the clematis.
Scarlet and bell shaped. Not thinking
of the consuming bacteria,
the small intestine.
Grief arrived.
The new absence—
it is best not to think of it. Collecting,
studying stamens and floral bracts instead.

II

The triumph of enduring art over ephemeral nature.

RELICS OF GLASS

For a moment each plant
unfolds,
blooming in stillness:
thistlelike heads,
fringed and curled petals.

Some of the blossoms are pale
                          like fossils.

THE PASSION FLOWER

The early European explorers believed it symbolized the Crucifixion:
fringe of the flowers representing Jesus' thorny crown.

The faithful apostles
                          Matthew, Thomas, Andrew, Simon the Zealot,
as the petals, the sepals.   The five stamens
Christ's wounded hands, feet, and right rib.

I think about religion often
                              while cold painting and wonder
how someone can believe that the knoblike stamens
resemble the nails that held Him to the cross.

MOST DAYS

I sleep on your side of the bed.
The dog and I count shadows—
some shaped like owls,
others like rhododendrons.

I write you letters on anything:
a window pane or cabbage leaf.
I left you a detailed account
of last Sunday on the shower curtain:

It's windy today.
The screen door needs fixing.
The carpenter bees have returned.

I stand in the garden
pulling petals.
Each one no longer united
at the base, but resting on my feet.

Do you know what I whisper to the scarlet corolla?
How I imagine your fingertips on the stem?

THE WATER LILIES

It is easy to forget the long crimson ropes that anchor
                              leaves and flower to muddy floors.
Rootstalks like Medusa's hair, serpentine and tangled.
Too often we are hypnotized by the surface
                            to understand what lies beneath it.

CONSIDER SOME FLOWERS

How threadyroots know their own paths,
coil, like wire or moon flower, around imaginary items:

Trellises. Wrists. Telephone poles.

It's only the glints of light
that give it all away:
the finest details are glass.

III

The triumph of form over matter.

GHOST PLANT

It is best to repeat the variation of colors.
Pale pink. Deep red. White.
They grow without sunlight—
exhumed from the earth like awkward bones.
I lose track of the alternate names.
It is like this with each one. At my work table
I think of the cold months. Each model
stunted in blossomed glory.
Sometimes I miss the beauty in wilting.

NINE FEET

The distance from one edge of the Matilija poppy to the other is six inches.
"The distance between the dead and the living
*   is more than a heartbeat and a breath."*
Or, as you told me in a dream, nine feet above our heads.

SECRET APPARATUS

There is none.
Calyx, corolla, stamen, petals.
I work with each by hand.
The only way to become a glass modeler of skill, I have often said to people,
     is to get a good great-grandfather who loved glass.
Liver leaf. Palo Cruz. Bloodflower. Bush Poppy.

AND I AM REMINDED HOW WE SLEPT

You and I
stirring like stems
of blue-eyed grass
before a storm, waking
some mornings
with our backs
unintentionally,
towards one another.

HOW TO DEFINE THINGS

Sometimes bougainvillea is called paper flower.
Sometimes bougainvillea is called bougainvillea.

WHAT I TELL THE WORKTABLE

The sixty-watt bulb beside the front door burned out days ago.
The street is empty except for the remains of a seagull—
                              wisps of feathers and bone.
Glass flowers don't need rain or soil. Roots
simply end. Abruptly.

WITHOUT

You have been absent so long that I almost expect something new—
a choir of bells, a porcelain soap dish, shadows on the wallpaper.

When the weatherman predicts rain, I remember the shape of your hands
and the way the switch grass grew that August,

each stem an extension pointing upwards,
each stalk bent slightly to the left towards the woods.

September would be an elegy: *It was warm that month.*
The rain never came. You were young.

Maybe it was all in the way things fell—azaleas from my hands,
a single Rosy Finch feather, yesterday's wash and all the clothespins, a star.

Additional Acknowledgements

Love and thanks to Mom and Dad—the first to read the poems I've written and for always being my biggest fans—I love you. Thank you, Paulette & Fred, for everything (especially for not thinking that a degree in Creative Writing was a silly idea). Love you both too. To Jenny, Andy and Julie for the support, advice, edits, and love. To everyone at Finishing Line Press, thank you for this amazing opportunity. Thanks to Mary Beth Wing, the first teacher who encouraged my poetry writing and to those teachers after, particularly the Creative Writing (Poetry) MFA faculty at Emerson College where this collection began (especially John Skoyles and Roy Kamada thank you, thank you). To Christian, who is missed every day. I cannot help but mention my grandparents who were the creative backbones of my family—Tenta, Nana Jane, Nana Priscilla & Brownie. I'm happy to follow in your footsteps and put some art into this world.

For Todd, Margaux and Weezie—my sun, my moon and stars, for always & always

Keena Boling's poetry has appeared in *The White Whale Review, Snow Jewel 2, The Writing Disorder, Grey Sparrow Press, The Furnace Review, Into the Teeth of the Wind,* and other print and online journals. A graduate of the MFA program at Emerson College, Keena was an English teacher at a small, private high school before taking time off to be with her children and focus more on writing. *Consider Some Flowers* was inspired by the famed "Glass Flowers" of the Ware Collection of Blaschka Glass Models of Plants at the Harvard Museum of Natural History and their creators, Leopold and Rudolf Blaschka. Keena lives in Boston with her husband and two daughters.

www.ingramcontent.com/pod-product-compliance
Lightning Source LLC
LaVergne TN
LVHW041519070426
835507LV00012B/1675